To colleen
Have fun
Sewing!
Lois

Pleats

...........contemporary use of pleated fabric

By LOIS ERICSON

DEDICATION: TO MY MOM ON HER 80TH

HAPPY BIRTHDAY, LILLY!

Photography: Carole Sesko
                Philip Ballantyne
Model: Carole Sesko
Calligraphy: Pamela Whitman
Drawings: Diane Ericson
Editor: Lennart Ericson
Special thanks to Kathy & Bets
    and my artist friends...Jonda,
    Ingrid & Madeline for their input.

ISBN # 0-911985 - 05- 0

PREFACE

This book is a natural consequence of Lois' great interest in fabrics and her very imaginative creativity as a designer. Full of examples, this innovative work will increase her following among fabric enthusiasts ......many of whom are so delighted with her books in this field. Her large file of fan letters with favorable comments are well deserved. When you see her collection of original creations, fashion design will have a new meaning for you. Until then you can see some of it on the pages that follow.

Lennart Ericson, Editor

INTRODUCTION

Pleats in various forms have always been a fascination for me. In this book, pleats will be 'investigated'....whether commercially pleated, pleated by hand or by using a smocking pleater. Using pleats in a contemporary way is THE focus of this book.

When I saw the smocking pleater for the first time....watching the fabric magically go in one end and come out at the other -- pleater and fabric 'in motion' -- I was practically in orbit! My mind was reeling with ideas for non-traditional use while the demonstrator was telling me how to straighten the rows exactly and to embroider a monotonous design on top of the pleats. I couldn't wait to take it home to see what some of the possibilities were going to be. I'd like to share some of my findings with you.

.............................Lois

CONTENTS

Types

In this book. . . several types of pleating will be reviewed and the methods to achieve the pleating will be discussed. I usually look toward finding easier ways of doing things to get the effect that I want. I will pass along the short-cuts and hints that I have discovered.

The most obvious short-cut is to purchase commercially pleated fabric. . . that may sound easy, but not as readily available as one might think. If fabric stores have it, very often it is found in the lingerie or formal/bridal department. If it is non-existent, you may have to be resourceful and pleat it yourself.

The easy way to obtain pleated fabric is to have your own material pleated for you. There are many pleating styles to choose from i.e. Box Pleats, Mushroom Pleats, Knife Pleats, Accordian Pleats and Crystal Pleats to name but a few. To find a pleating company, see the suppliers list also in the phone books of larger cities, check the yellow pages for pleating services.

One way to pleat your own fabric is with a smocking pleater *. It is available in various widths and is very easy to use. The size of the pleats is not adjustable but these small pleats can be used in a variety of ways. . . as you will soon see.

Another method to make pleats is to use an ingenious easy -to-use device called Perfect Pleater*. The pleats can be 1/4, 1/2 or 3/4 inch or wider. . . or in combination of those sizes. I rarely do any thing symmetrical so I like that option.

*See Suppliers, Page 76.

Methods

Smocking Pleater.

When you hear the word smocking --- the usual visual picture is one of children's clothes decorated with cute designs lovingly embroidered on them. A very time consuming process to be sure. To take this technique and put it into a contemporary concept, I have devised a method to give dimension and texture to a garment. The result is very 'grown-up' and the garments are definitely one-of-a-kind. Using a smocking pleater makes the gathering/basting process a fast and easy one.

When acquiring a new piece of equipment, i.e. the smocking pleater, it is very important to learn all you can about it and to give yourself permission to play. By trying different ideas you will multiply the possibilities when you combine them with the techniques that you already know.

The smocking pleater will be referred to from now on as simply the 'pleater'. It will be easier to use your pleater if you clamp it to the table with a 'C' clamp or a spring-type clamp.

Suggestion: try pleating some small pieces of various kinds of fabric, to see the results. Roll the fabric on a 1/2" dowel that is at least 6" longer than the pleater. Place the end of the material in between the two large gears, turn the handle clockwise and Voila. . . the fabric comes out onto the needles then onto the threads --- pleated.

Many weights of fabric can be used with the pleater. In addition to the traditional ones. . . I have tried many silks i.e., organza, noil, tussah. . . wools i.e., challis, crepe. . . also handkerchief linen and lightweight pinwale corduroy. Keep in mind that the fabrics that pleat easily are soft, sheer, flimsy, pliable and loose woven. If there is any doubt about your choice of fabrics, cut a narrow strip and feed it into the pleater. If it is difficult to turn the handle, choose another material. The pleater will not break but some needles probably will, if the fabric is unsuitable.

If a fabric is too thick or tightly woven it will be difficult to turn the handle. If the fabric is already rolled on the dowel and it is in the pleater when you discover that it is not going to work, rather than break many of the needles , simply loosen the two screws and lift out the removable gear. Take out the fabric and the needles. Replace the needles.

Speaking of breaking needles, here are some tips to help keep the needles in good working order. Cut off the selvages, the tight weave on the selvage edge can be a strain on the needles and can cause them to break. It is best to avoid sewing seams before pleating. The extra thickness can be just enough to break the needles. Washable fabrics should be washed first to eliminate sizing and make it more supple. The needles need to be sharp and smooth for best results. To lubricate the needles, run a narrow strip of waxed paper through the pleater occasionally.

The pleats in many synthetics, wools and silks can be heat set. That means that the pleats can be permanent. Many of the synthetics will keep the pleats through handwashing, (drip dry). The silks and wools may have to be dry cleaned. To heatset. . . tie the threads, push the pleats against the knots so the pleats are very tight. Steam press. To help set the pleats, use a pressing cloth, dipped in a mixture of nine parts water with one part white vinegar.

The first thing to be done is to thread the needles. One of the main differences between traditional smocking and my approach (I call Nearly Smocked). . . is that I leave the basting threads in the fabric. They become one of the design elements. . . so the threads contrast or match the material. I also have the basting threads double so they are stronger and won't break as easily. Most any sewing machine thread works well. Very fine elastic thread is good to experiment with also. Note: Allow 2 1/2 to 3 times the width when pleating your fabric this way, to assure adequate fullness.

Place the pleater on a table with the handle facing out towards you. Start threading the needles with the one farthest from you first --- so you don't work across the ones already threaded. Double the thread, and tape the threads at the other end of the table. It's great to have a long table so the pleater doesn't have to be threaded so often.

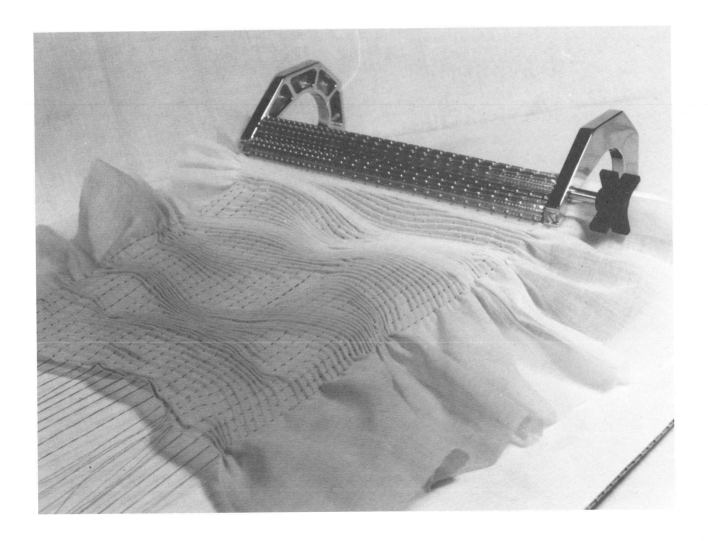

As the stripes, placed vertically, are pleated, they are moved from side to side as the handle is turned. The result is a multiple "W" design similar to a flame stitch in embroidery.

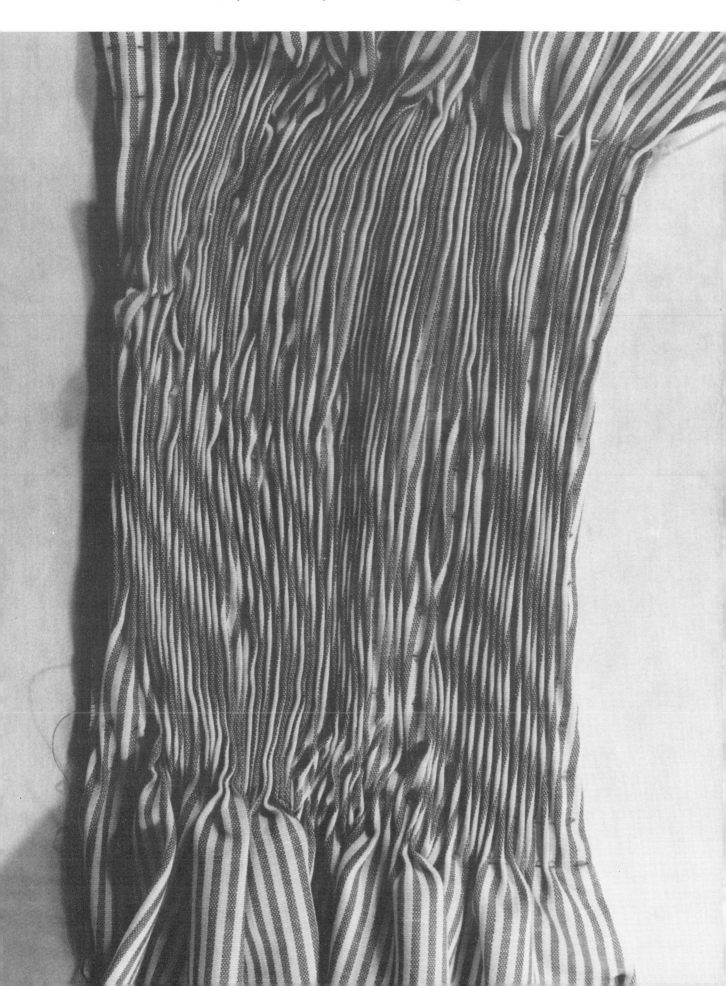

Pin stripes can be a subtle choice. The combination of the bias cut and the contrasting basting thread make this an eye-catching example.

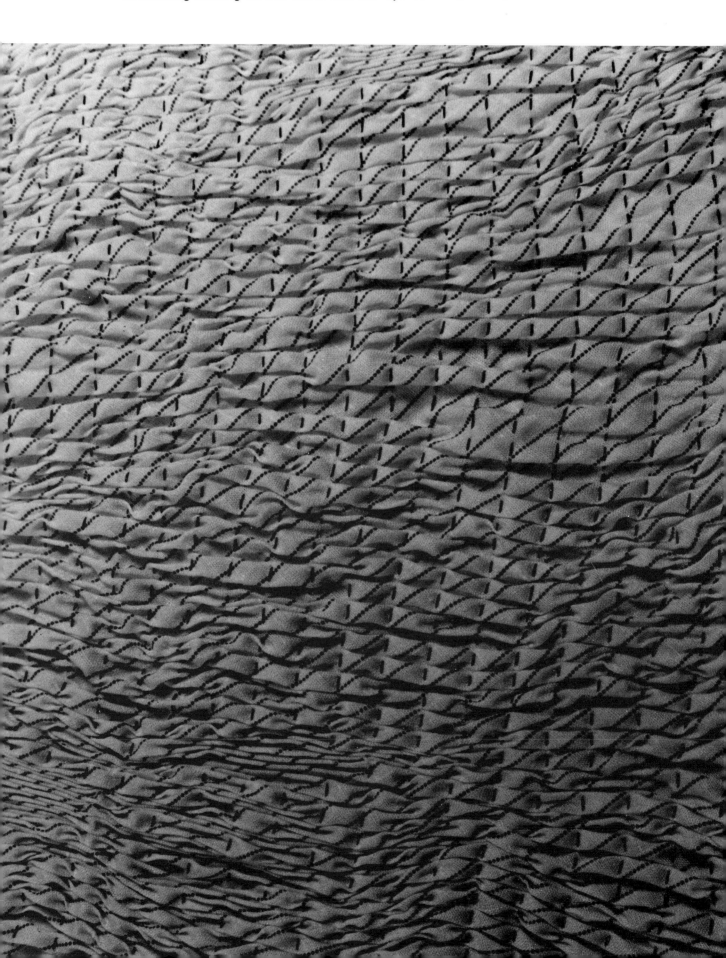

There are 24 needles on this particular smocking pleater. It isn't necessary to thread them all...just as many as desired. The threaded ones need not be in any particular order. Notice that the spaces left unthreaded become puffy. The open spaces could also be stuffed or pressed flat.   13

Try stuffing sections of pleated fabric with small shapes i.e. beads or spheres of batting or foam rubber. The shapes are fastened by wrapping thread around the base and securing. Extra folds then occur to create additional texture. 14

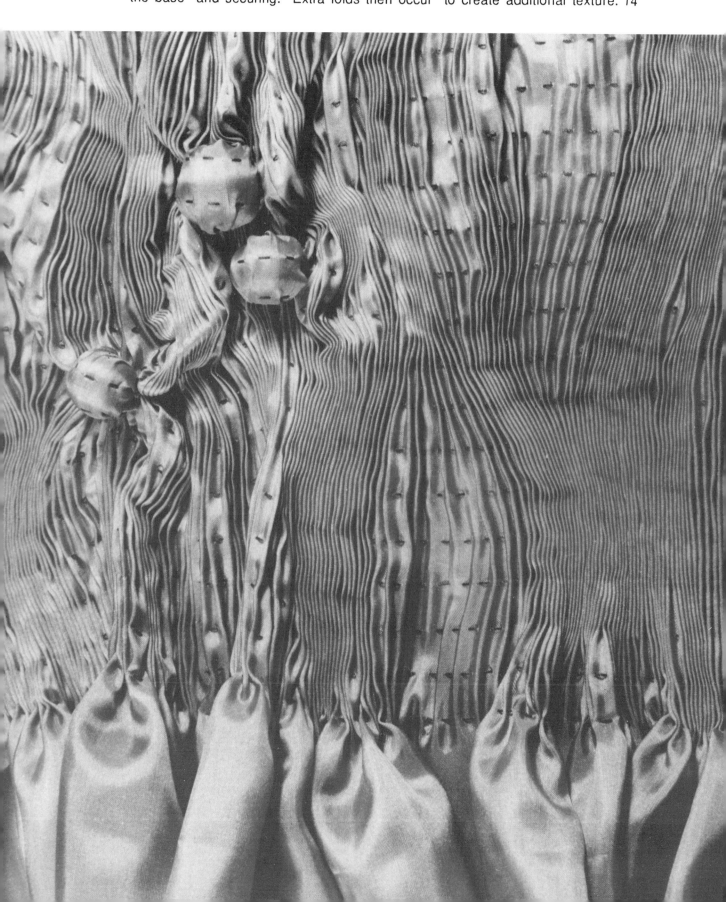

When a fabric is plain, especially if it is fairly thin ...consider making perpendicular folds in the material as it is inserted into the pleater. The texture of the folds, combined in the pleats, makes this an interesting option.15

Pleating is a good technique to use when adding texture to smooth knits. Knits are available in many weights so it would be adviseable to choose a lightweight one for this particular method.   16

Open mesh or gauze fabrics can be provocative choices. When densely pleated,
the character of the material changes completely.   17

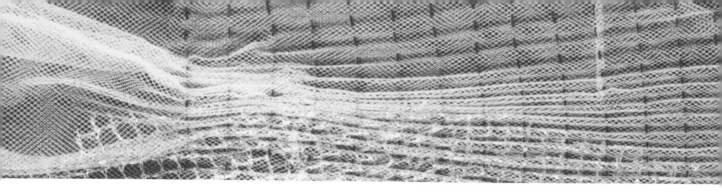

Sheers, i.e. organza, tulle, net, mesh... could all be used in this example. Sheers are a good choice to eliminate bulk, as there are several layers here. The sheers also let the colored shapes show through. These colored shapes are sandwiched between two layers of tulle, then pleated.   18

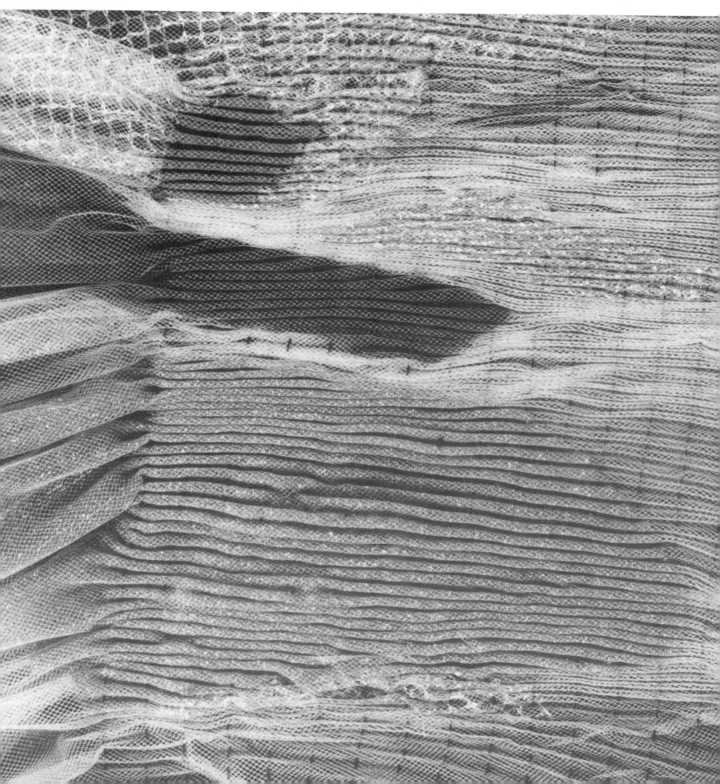

This sheer fabric has been run through the pleater two times, one perpendicular to the other. Since the basting threads are always a part of the design element...consider the color of the threads as they cross each other. 19

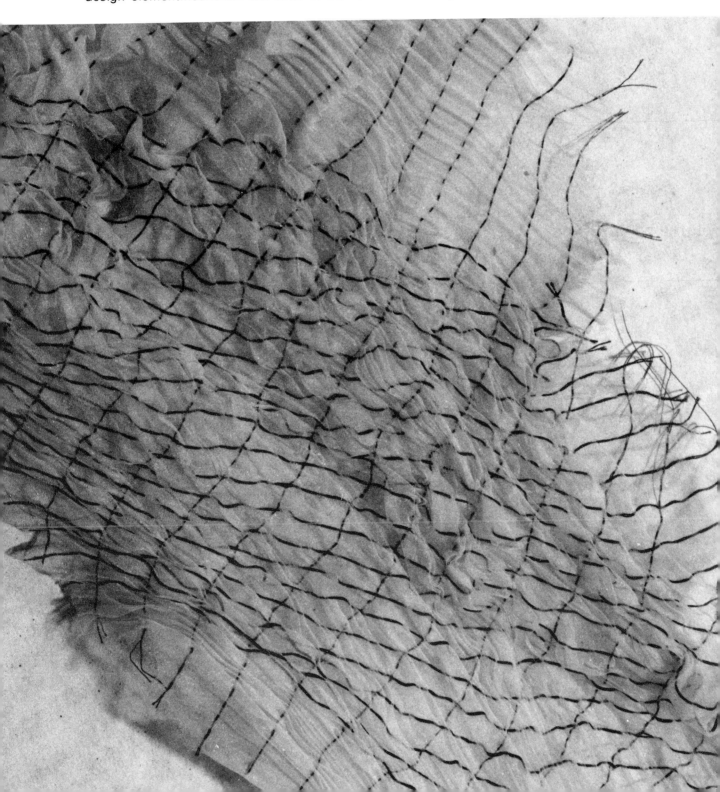

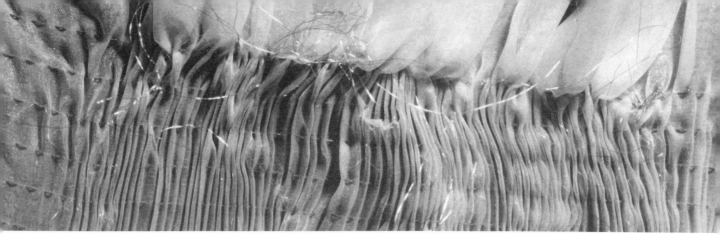

Thin copper wire is sandwiched between two layers of organza, then pleated. The basting threads hold layers together and the wire in place. The wire would not be a good choice for use in clothing but great for wall pieces or sculpture since it could be molded into shapes. Other additions for use in clothing could be yarn, ribbon, threads, unspun fleece or ?. 20

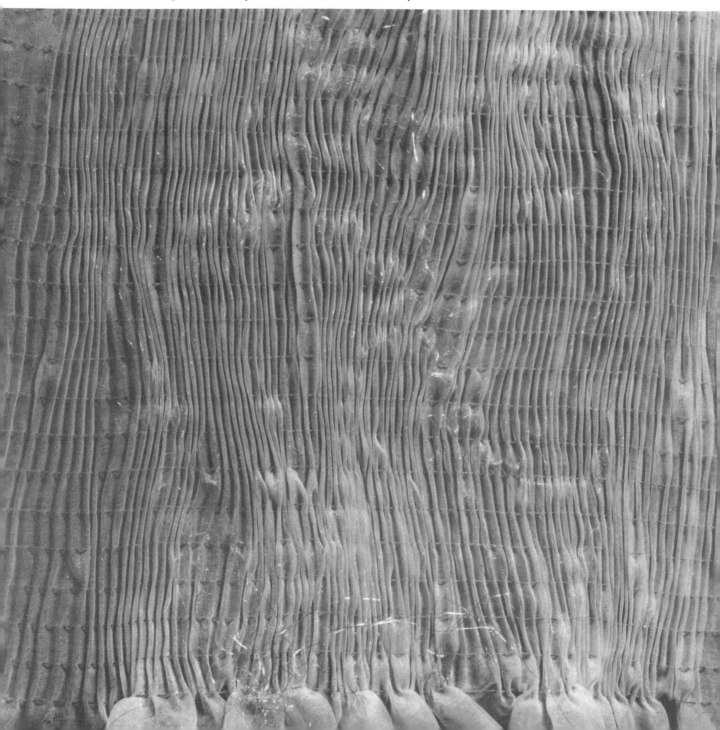

This metallic fabric, when pleated, will reflect the light.

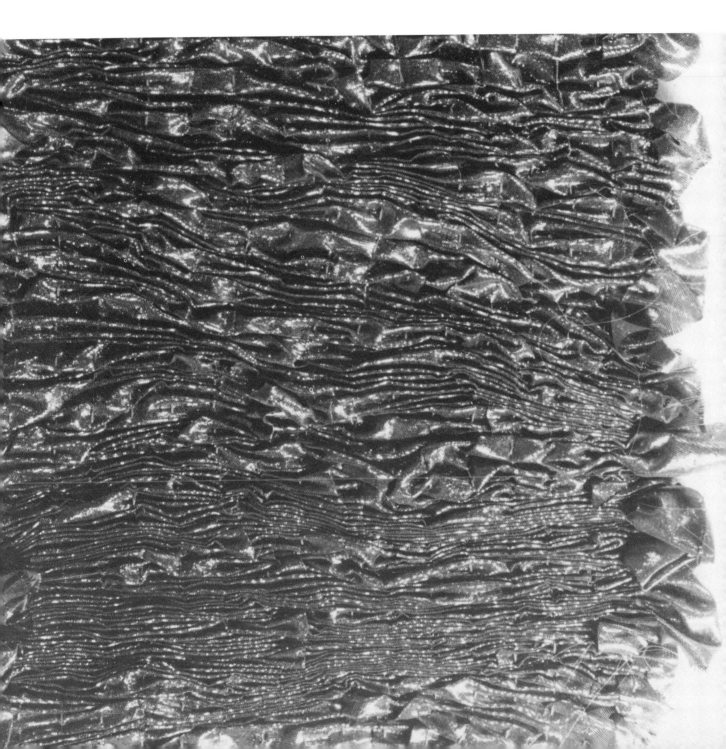

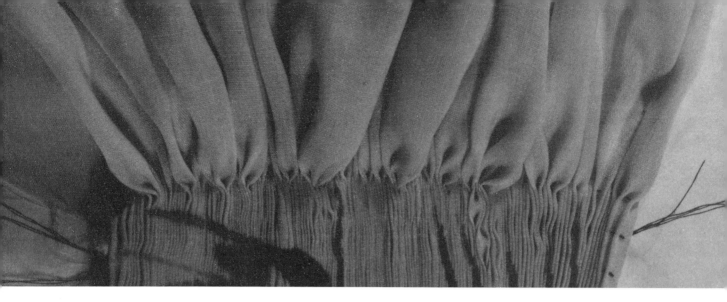

If the surface of the pleating is to be painted, here is a great technique. The basting threads are pulled tight and the threads tied together at one end. Gather the fabric in tight and tie off the other ends of the basting threads, to keep them condensed. Now paint the fabric as desired.   22

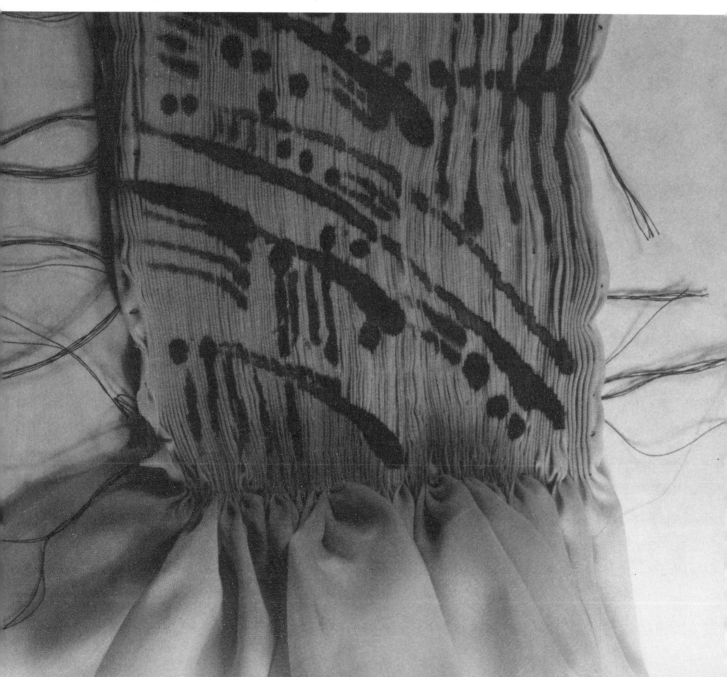

After the paint is dry and the fabric has been heat set, pull out the basting threads. The fabric can be ironed flat, if desired.   23

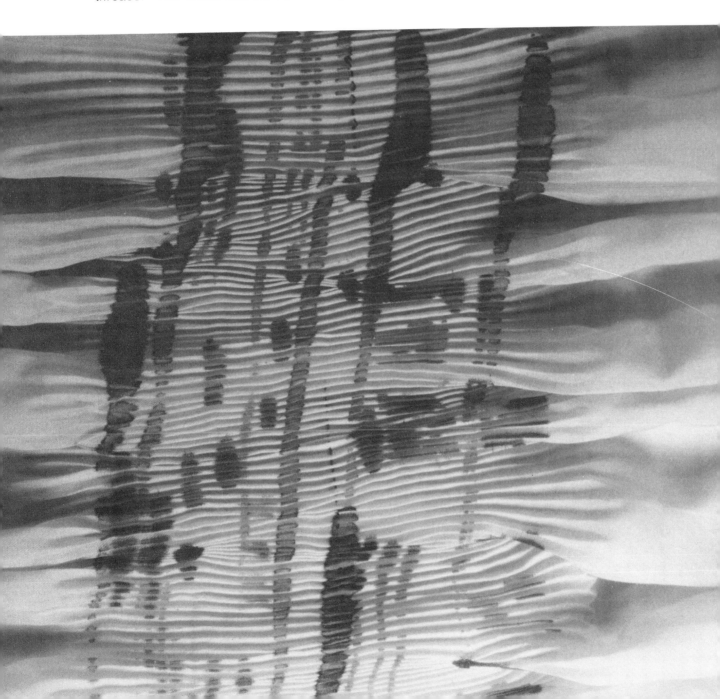

Perfect Pleater.

The Perfect Pleater is an easy to use device. The fabric is tucked in the louvers and steam pressed in place.

To use, place the Perfect Pleater on the ironing board with the open louvers away from you. Tuck the fabric into the louvers with your fingers, being careful to push the material in all the way. Using the linen setting on the iron and a damp pressing cloth, press in the pleats. To help set the pleats (even better) use a pressing cloth that has been wet with the vinegar/water mixture.

Very Important --- leave the fabric in the Perfect Pleater until cool.

To hold the pleats in place as the fabric is removed from the Perfect Pleater. . . use a narrow strip of iron-on interfacing at each end of the pleats, or basting tape. If the fabric is wider than the Perfect Pleater, you may wish to stitch the pleats after pressing/cooling and before removing from the Perfect Pleater. Sometimes I place the fabric right side down and press a fuseable interfacing on the wrong side. Allow to cool, when the fabric is removed. . . the right side looks like tucks.

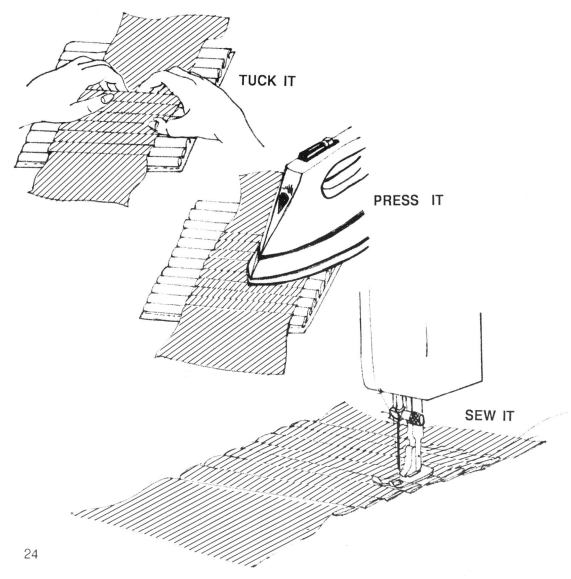

TUCK IT

PRESS IT

SEW IT

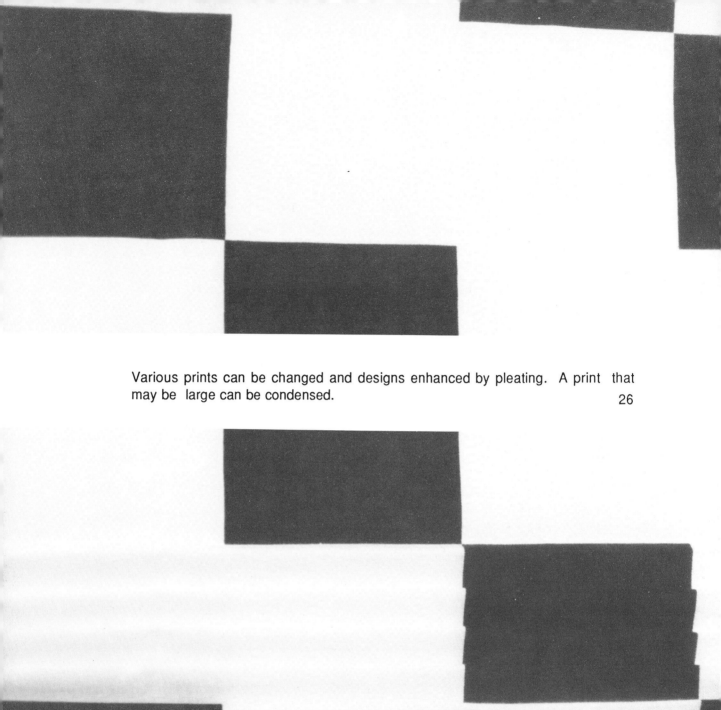

Various prints can be changed and designs enhanced by pleating. A print that may be large can be condensed.   26

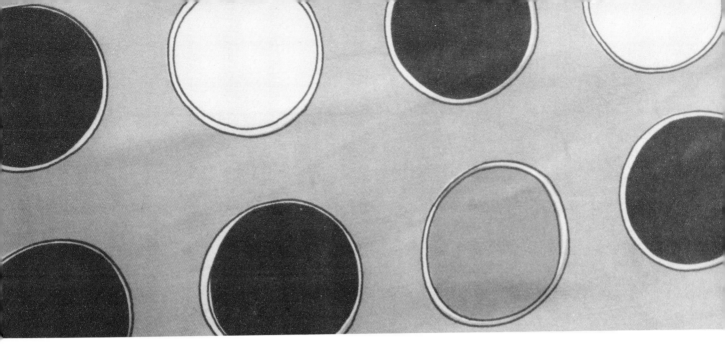

A monotonous print can be made more interesting. The folds create dimension and movement.

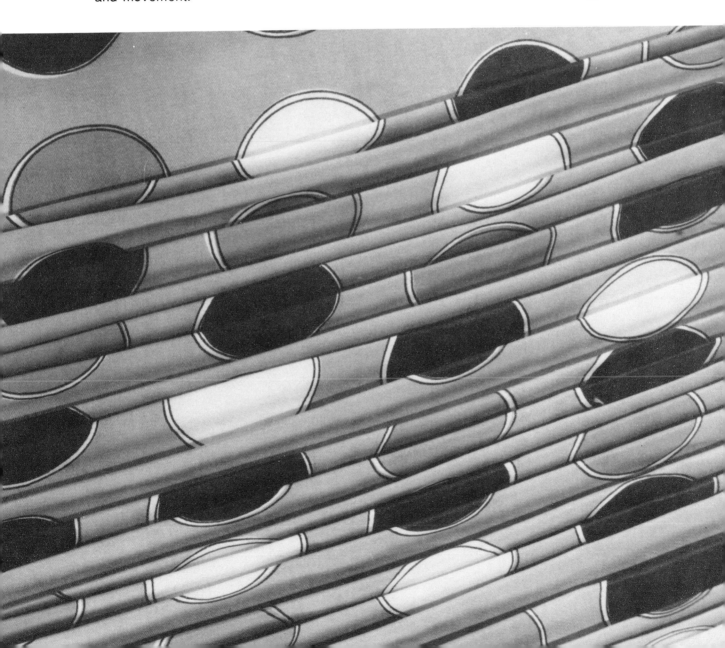

Stripes become even more wonderful whether cut on the bias or straight. Remember to allow extra fabric if using it on the bias for pleating.   28

Interrupted stripes seem to stop and start as though printed with this process
'in mind'.

This bold chevron pattern results in an optical illusion when pleated.

30

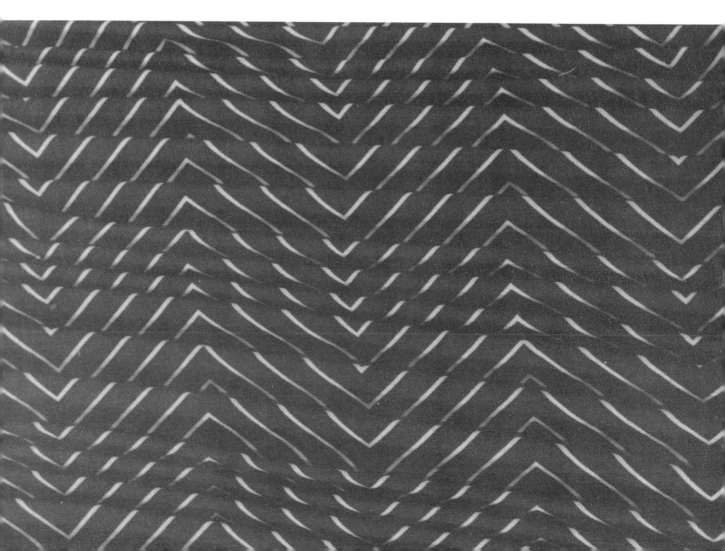

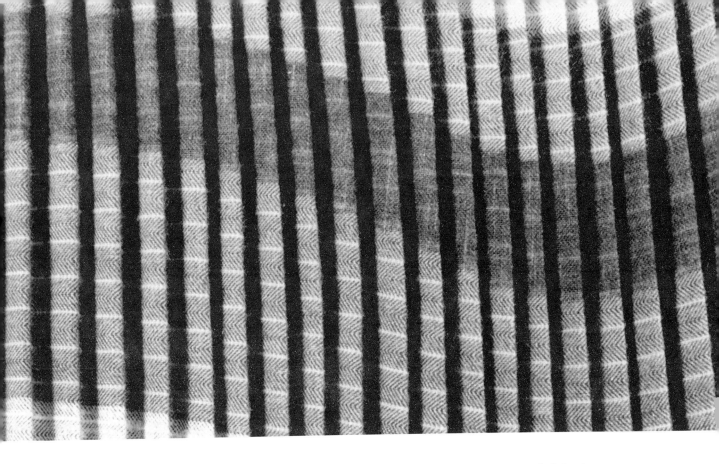

As a striped fabric is pleated...it is possible to move each row slightly to create undulating stripes.

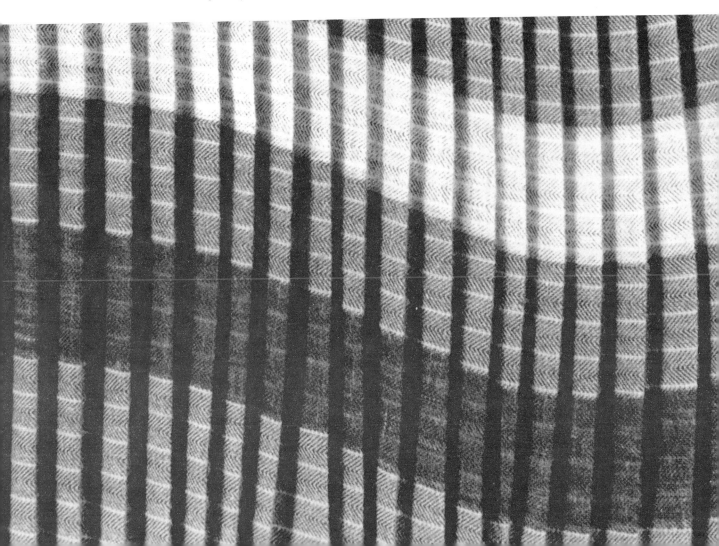

This cotton material has been silk-screened and then pleated. The printed
bands of color create the movement of the pattern.   32

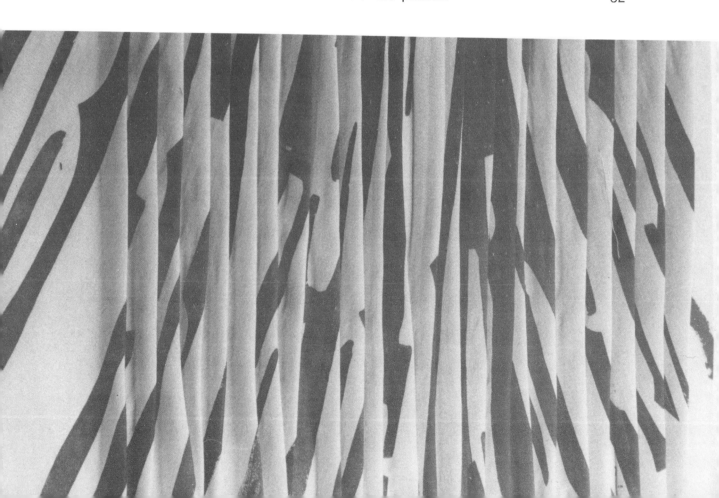

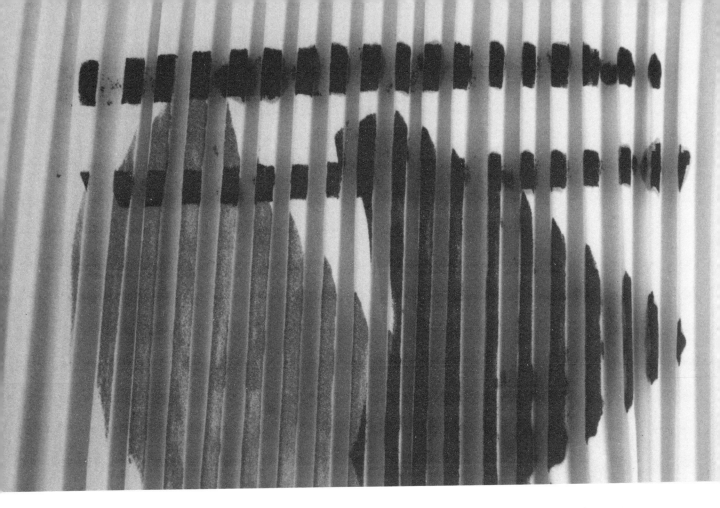

Stencilling (or painting) on top of the pleats is the method used for this sample. The design can be spread apart as much or as little as desired. So if fabric painting is one of interest, combine it with the pleating for another option.   33

One way to create folds on the pleats is to fold the fabric as desired and press. Place the folded fabric on the Perfect Pleater and pleat. Set as usual. 34

The result, of this striped cotton, is one of movement and directional changes of the stripes.   It was amazing to me how dimensional the result was on this sample.

Another method to create additional texture to the pleats is to fold the fabric
AS it is pleated. Make small folds in the fabric and pleat. Set as usual.   36

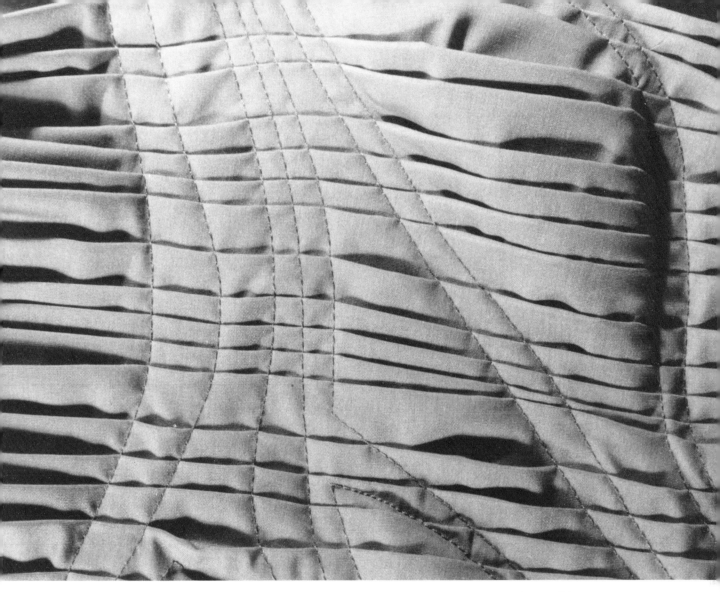

To create a bas-relief effect, cut shapes of foam rubber or batting. Then apply these shapes to a base material with fabric glue. Place the pleated cotton on top and pin. The machine stitching emphasizes the shapes and keeps all the layers together.

Pieces of material, ribbon or lace can be stitched onto the base fabric to create a design before pleating. Cut the shapes, serge or hem, if desired. In this sample, sheer black bias strips are sewn to a silver and black nylon fabric, then pleated and set as usual. The pleating re-aligns the design in an interesting way.

38

Printed bias tape is sewn to linen fabric, then pleated.

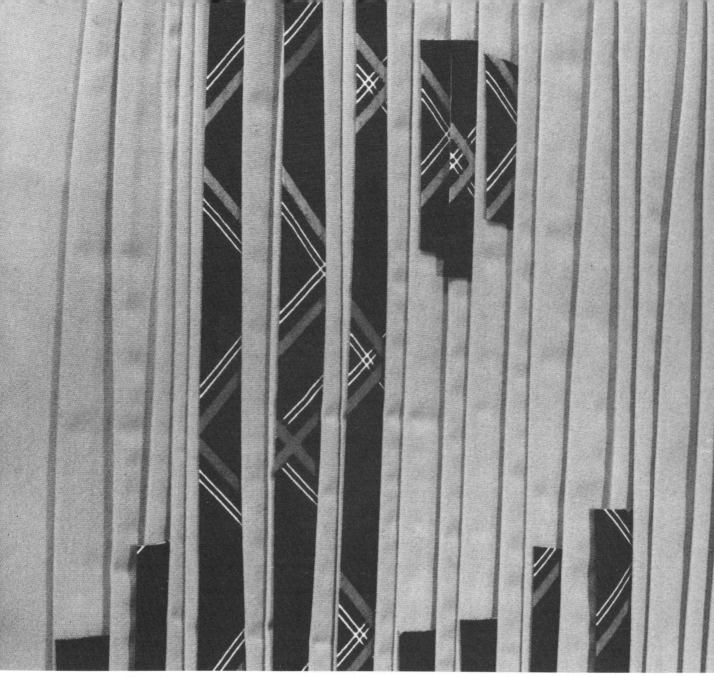

After the pleats are pressed in and 'set', printed bias sections are inserted in the pleats. The insertions can be sewn 'invisibly' by lifting the pleat that is covering the insert and machine stitching to keep in place. Wonderful designs and movement are possible to create with the placement of the inserts.

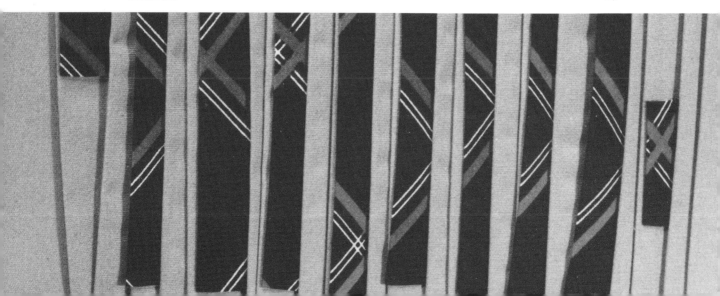

There are many ways to keep the pleats in place. This example show how to use ribbons or tapes arranged in a grid pattern, then stitched. 41

Striped tussah silk is cut on the bias and pleated. The curved satin stitching lines keep the pleats in place and yet leave the pleats free to 'move'.   42

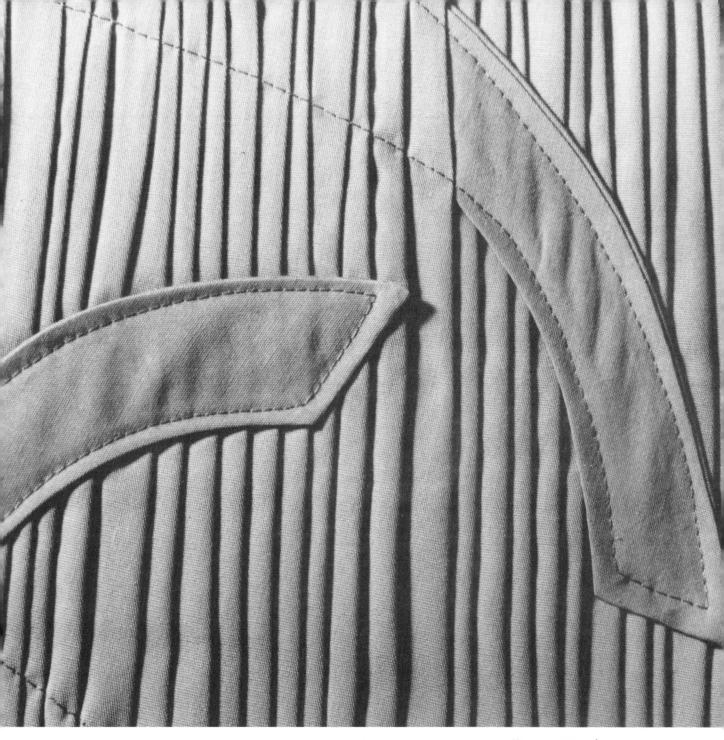

Small faced shaped are stitched to hold the pleats in place. These curved shapes are cut and stitched to a facing fabric. The shapes are trimmed, turned, and pressed to complete each small unit. Place the faced shapes on the pleats and topstitch.   43

Striped cotton is placed on the bias and pleated. A facing is stitched in the desired shape, in this case, a diamond. The hole is cut-out, corners clipped, the facing turned. Another piece of the pleated stripes is placed in back of the faced hole. All are stitched together.

Darts can be a decorative element as well as a structural one. In this case, fabric that has been pleated is inserted in the darts...or it could be inserted in seams, as well. The pleated fabric is cut into shapes. The edges to be exposed are finished with bias. The unfinished edges are inserted into the dart or seam. Additional darts without inserts are stitched to repeat the design. 45

The pattern for the wedges is made by cutting a circle into 8ths. Place and pin the wedges to a pleated rectangle of fabric. Machine stitch around each wedge. Cut out each wedge very close to the stitching.

In addition to the circle, try placing these wedges in various configurations. Play with the shapes. These wedges can be faced with bias strips or finished with machine satin stitching when appliqued in place.　　　47

This cotton had narrow tucks woven in the fabric to begin with, so when it is pleated on the diagonal it adds even more interest.

Using the pleater on lace makes it easy to apply to curves, i.e. collars, cuffs. Pleated lace can also be inserted in tucks or combined with strip piecing.   49

Serging the edges of the pleated fabric and layering them is another possibility.

Shapes are cut in a melton wool, which is perfect for this idea since the wool doesn't ravel. These cut shapes become the finished edge, and are placed on top of the pleated cotton. The stitching holds the layers together and emphasizes the shapes of the cut holes.

This silk fabric is painted, then pleated. Basting stitches are tied on one side and pulled tight. Use a pressing cloth dipped in the vinegar and water mixture to set the pleats.

When the threads are removed, the very narrow pleats are set-in. This may be a permanent 'condition' in a polyester or some of the other man-made fabrics. Suggestion: pleat and hand-wash a trial sample to assure the desired result.

The yoke section on a wool coat is pleated. The fabric is placed wrong side up in the pleater. An iron-on interfacing is applied after the pleating process. The rows of pleats are machine stitched in alternating directions.

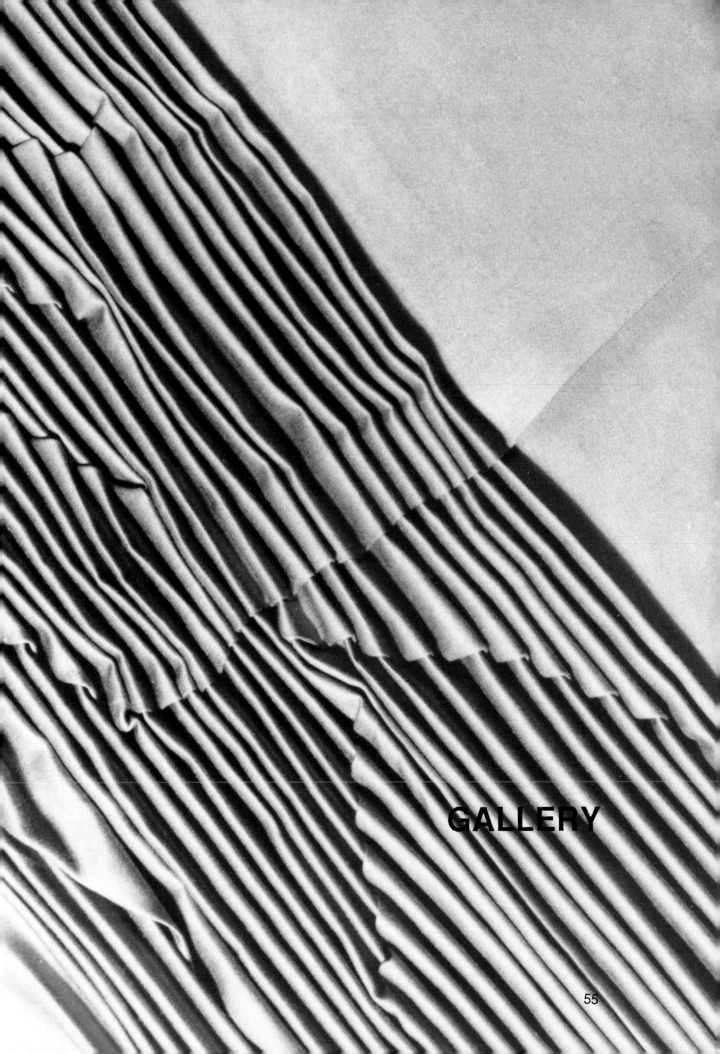

GALLERY

"When you create something and it's all yours, it doesn't get any better than that."

L. McCrum

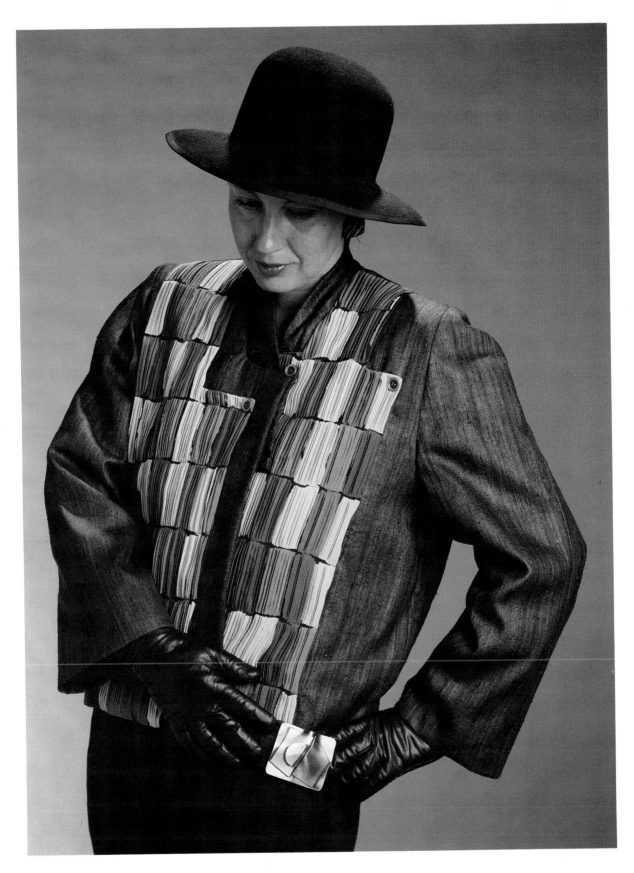

GALLERY REFERENCES

The photographs in the Gallery section are by Gary Jameson, with the exception of 60, 62 & 71. All the garments in this section are by the author with the two exceptions noted.

Striped silk and cotton fabric is cut to accentuate the large pleated collar. This black collar is a rectangle that is folded in half to create the fan shape. The collar is versatile and can be worn in a variety of ways. Pleating by State Pleating   57

Blue cotton in a twill weave is the fabric for this 3/4 coat with a short pleated jacket worn on top. The pleated panels, front and back, are stitched in a curved design. The tape (from the 30's or 40's) with little buttons on it, is sewn on by hand.   58

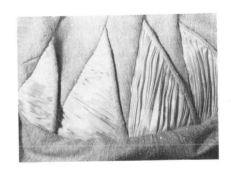

Commercially pleated fabric is cut into wedges. To finish one long side of these triangular wedges, a facing has been applied to that side. The other long side, an unfinished edge, is inset in a dart and stitched. The short side of the wedge is at the cap edge of the sleeve. Sleeves are a wonderfully 'neutral' space to make the point of interest.... a consideration. Pleating by State Pleating   59

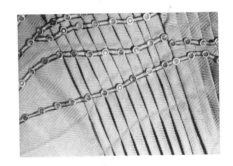

The linen yardage is randomly pleated, then the very edge of the pleats is stitched...creating a small tuck. The pattern pieces are cut out and underlined. It needs no ironing and has a wonderful permanently wrinkled look.
Artist: Charlotte Reinhardt (Delmar NY)   60

Herringbone wool in shades of grey with threads of mauve and blue is the fabric choice for this short jacket. The back yoke and the front are pleated on the Perfect Pleater. These areas are stitched on in a random pattern with the matching mauve and blue threads to hold the pleats in place. The back of the jacket, below the yoke, is pleated and the pleats are loose. Covered cording and antique metal buttons finish the front and cuffs.   61

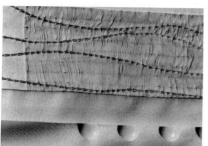

The fabric is organza, the 'tool' is the smocking pleater, the effect is subtle and classic. After pleating the fabric, it is inset in a cream colored shantung, the main fabric of the jacket. Chain stitches in grey, are sewn in a linear design. The stitching starts on the pleated sections and continues on the heavier material.
Artist: Karen Perrine (Tacoma, Wa.)   62

The pleats on this navy, wine and cream striped fabric are manipulated and machine stitched to hold in place. The closure is lapis and silver.   63

The teal colored silk is commercially pleated in a mushroom pattern. The blouse is mainly a rectangle with faced armholes. A cording, sewn on at the neckline, ties at the back. The collar can be worn in a variety of ways. Pleating by San Francisco Pleating
                                                              64

The pleats on the yoke, of the silk sleeveless coat, are folded back and forth, then stitched to hold in place. The sections of pleats and the shapes on the lower portions of the coat are faced with satin to emphasize the shapes. A dress with a bias cut cowl neckline, straight skirt and dressy belt also in shades of mauve is not shown.   In the collection of Barbi Racich   65

Ruffles are made easily and evenly on the smocking pleater. Only three or four needles are threaded on the pleater to make the ruffles on this organza and antique lace blouse.   66

The crepe-de-chine fabric is commercially pleated in a mushroom pleating pattern. The square print is accentuated by the shape of the facings that are stitched to the charcoal tussah silk. A wide belt with a contemporary buckle fastens the jacket.
Pleating by San Francisco Pleating   67

The sleeves on this top are cut extra wide, so there is 2 1/2 to 3 times the size of the cuff to pleat. The pleated fabric is stitched to an underlining to stabilize on both the cuffs and collar. Thread loops and antique metal buttons finish this long dressy shirt, worn with reversible silk pants.   68

Ikat silk is the choice for this shirt/jacket with pleated yoke and cuffs. To fasten, covered cording is wound around the garment shaped porcelain button. 69

Pleats (3/4") are manipulated and stitched to hold in place on this unlined wool coat. The very full sleeves end in a pleated cuff. A separate cuff with a straight sleeve would, of course, take less fabric.   70

Striped silk is pleated on the bias for an unusual effect. Using it on the bias takes a little more fabric but the result is definitely worth it. The satin stitching, in a curved design, holds the pleats in place while keeping the flexibility intact.   71

This silk tussah is pleated with the Perfect Pleater. The pleats are machine stitched with one of the shades in the multi-colored weave. Utilizing the option of varying the size of the pleats is very evident in this coat. Some of the spaces are left unpleated. The wide band/collar is quilted and machine stitched.   72

SUPPLIERS

PLEATING COMPANIES

A-1 Pleating
8426 1/2 W. 3rd. St.
Los Angeles, Ca. 90048
(213) 653-5557
Custom pleating, any combination possible. If you can imagine it, they can
pleat it. 2,000 choices.

Koppel Pleating
890 Garrison
Bronx, N.Y. 10474
(212) 893-1500
In addition to pleating, this company also offers tucking and shirring
services. Mention this book or Lois Ericson and you will receive a 10%

San Francisco Pleating
425 Second St. 5th Floor Dept. R.
San Francisco, Ca. 94107
(415) 982-3003
Send for a free brochure.

State Pleating
582 "E" St.
So. Boston, Mass. 02210
(617) 426-1986
This company has 3,000 different pleating patterns, also ask for a 10%
discount for mentioning this book or Lois Ericson.

PLEATERS:

Devices to pleat the fabric yourself.

Perfect Pleater: (P&H 2.00)	$24.00
Smocking pleaters: 24 row Stanley Pleater (P&H 5.00)	$125.00
Extra Needles, per dozen	9.00

Note: these prices good thru December, 1989....write for a new price list
after that date.

For other books by Lois Ericson please refer to the order form at the back
of the book.

AUTHOR

After viewing my work and books, a lady once asked, "how does your mind work, anyway:" I have enjoyed being a little different but I never thought in those terms , I guess.

Straying from traditional use of techniques has never been my obvious goal, but it seems to be the direction my work takes....looking at one thing and seeing another. Being able to visualize is helpful, also I enjoy experimenting and I give myself permission to play.

I'm often asked if I have any 'idols'. Oh, yes! My all time favorite is Erte'. In the last 5 or 6 years Issey Miyake has been a strong influence. What a great artist he is. Georgia O'keefe and Louise Nevelson have been inspirational, not only for their art but for their philosophy as well.

Lois Ericson
Box 1680
Tahoe City, Ca. 95730

In the studio, looking for the right button in my terrific 'stash'.....

Lois...........

Thank you for the inspiration. I so often ask myself why I ever hold back. You always remind me of the joy when I go for it.

.............Flo

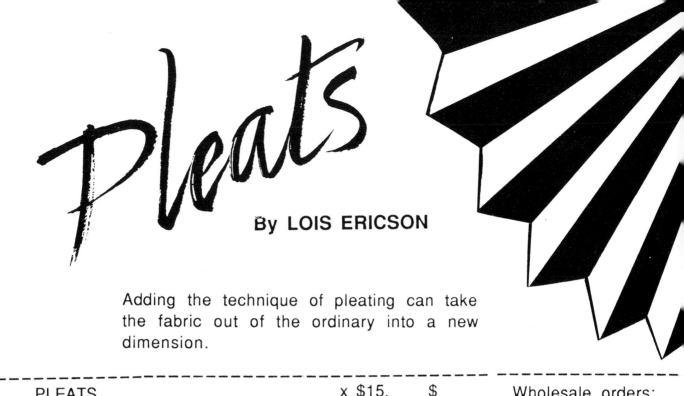

Pleats

By LOIS ERICSON

Adding the technique of pleating can take the fabric out of the ordinary into a new dimension.

PLEATS	_____ x $15.	$_____	Wholesale orders:
TEXTURE....a closer look	_____ x $22.	$_____	12 or more books,
DESIGN & SEW IT YOURSELF. . .	_____ x $15.	$_____	Mixed Titles
FABRICS....RECONSTRUCTED. . .	_____ x $14.	$_____	Discount: 40%
BELTS....WAISTED SCULPTURE.	_____ x $12.	$_____	Plus P&H, net 30
PRINT IT YOURSELF.	_____ x $ 7.	$_____	SEND RESALE #, IF ORDERING WHOLE‑SALE

Cal. res. add 6% sales tax . . . .$_____

P&H $2.50 (1 to 3 books) . . . .$_____

TOTAL . . . .$_____

_____PLEASE SEND WORKSHOP INFORMATION.

CANADIAN CUSTOMERS - POSTAL MO OR CHECKS ON U..S.. BANKS, PLEASE.

MAIL CHECK OR MO TO:

LOIS ERICSON
BOX 1680
TAHOE CITY, CA. 95730

NAME _____

ADDRESS_____

CITY_____STATE___ZIP_____

PERFECT PLEATER @ $24.   _____
  P&H . . . $2.00

SMOCKING PLEATER
    24 ROW STANLEY @$125.   _____
    EXTRA NEEDLES $9. per dozen _____
  P&H . . . $5.00
  Cal. res. add 6% sales tax

NOTE:
These prices are good thru 1989, after that, please write to me for the current prices.